ST. GEORGE

PRINCE OF MARTYRS

In loving memory of Yeshemabet Mennen, my sweet babe, whose angelic life was short lived, like the daughters of Beirut. Rest on in Paradise. T.R.

Thanks to my family and everyone who encouraged and supported me in accomplishing my mission, especially my son, Deacon Youhannes, Dalila Woodruff, and my dear friend Heather Green. I greatly appreciate the help I received from Merigeta Afework and Abba Yosef Berhane, who both told me about the life of St. George. Some of the stories I heard were from the Amharic Text, *Gelde Giorgis* (Gebreselassie, 1984)[i]. Thanks to Fanaye of Site Media, who was so patient and supportive in adding the finishing touch.

Copyright © 2012 by Tsionawit Rutty

All rights reserved. This book or any portion thereof may not be reproduced or used in any manner whatsoever without the express written permission of the publisher except for the use of brief quotations in a book review.

Printed in the United States of America

First Printing, 2012

ISBN 978-1-105-62417-9

Yeshemabet Publishing

yeshemabetpublishing@hotmail.com

Illustrations were done in oil paintings on goat skin, and photographed for the book.

Graphic design by Sitemedia.us

I thank God that through His help I have now fulfilled my promise, and am able to share the importance of St. George's life to Christianity. I hope this may serve as an inspiration to those who read this story to be vigilant and courageous as Christian soldiers.

[i]

To the memory of Archbishop Yesehaq, who taught me about St. George and other Ethiopian saints. As Archbishop of the Ethiopian Orthodox Tewahedo Church in the Western Hemisphere and Southern Africa, he stood steadfast in defending the Christian faith. He was, and still remains an inspiration in the lives of so many people. T.R.

Introduction

Saint George was born in the 3rd century in Lydda, known today as Lod in Israel. He was a valiant Christian knight known for his bravery, and stood strong, fearlessly, and unwavering in defense of his Christian faith. St. George could not be persuaded into worshipping idols. For this reason he suffered violent persecution at the hands of the governor Dudianus and his companions, who were idolaters. St. George embodied Christianity. He was blessed for his devotion by Our Lord Jesus Christ who visited him during his times of challenge, and most importantly, times of torture. He comforted him and assured him that after seven years of suffering, dying three times and coming back to life, he would enter into the kingdom of heaven on his fourth death. St. George patiently endured all his trials with courage.

Some of St. George's faithful friends stayed with him and recorded his sufferings. After his martyrdom, two of his disciples took his body back to his home town as he had previously requested. The tomb of St. George presently lies in the St. George Greek Orthodox Church in Lod, Israel.

I visited this church. Here visitors will discover a chain which is symbolically displayed as a reminder of the tortures inflicted upon St. George, including the times he suffered from being placed in chains. According to the Ethiopian priest who accompanied me, the custom is to have visitors put the chain on and then make a promise. I put the chain on, and my promise was to write this book.

St. George has always been my favorite saint, who I first learned about in elementary school. As an Ethiopian Orthodox Tewahedo Christian I have always prayed to him, believing in his protection, even when I knew very little of his greatness, and the many miracles that happened through him. Since I started on this mission, I have learned much more of this saint and his life. This knowledge has clearly served to increase my love of him and my personal quest to honor his holy life.

This glorious saint is revered by many Christians throughout the world. Celebrants other than Ethiopia include countries such as Egypt, England, Georgia, Russia, Greece, Beirut, and several others. In Ethiopia St. George is called Mar Giorgis. Mar is a title for holy people and also means honey (sweet). The departure of St. George is commemorated annually in Ethiopia on Miyaza 23rd Ethiopian (Julian) calendar, which is May 1st on the Gregorian calendar.

The trials of St. George were much more than I have mentioned in this brief account, and my words are insufficient to express the omnipotence of God revealed through the miracles surrounding the life of this holy man, chosen and blessed by God to be the Prince of Martyrs.

* * * * * * *

There was a man in the country of Cappadocia in Rome called Gerontius*. By the will of God he traveled to Palestine. When he arrived in Palestine, Gerontius was quite attracted to this country, deeply loving her in his heart. He was pleased with the beauty and fertility of the land, with its tall trees and olive oil which he felt tasted sweeter than that of any other country.

There was in Palestine a province called Lydda. Gerontius loved this country more than his own native land because this country was holy, sanctified by the feet of St. Peter who had walked through Lydda performing miracles and preaching the Gospel. One notable miracle was St. Peter healing a man who had been sick for eight years (Acts 9:32-35). After the people saw this miracle they converted to Christianity, and for this reason Gerontius liked to live in Lydda.

It was also the will of God for Gerontius to live there in order for his son, the blessed Saint George, to be born there. Mar (holy) George, the star of happiness, the star of honor, the star of teaching for those who traveled on the path to the kingdom of heaven. Saint George was the leader of the stars of martyrs who endured struggles for the name of our Lord Jesus Christ, until they entered the kingdom of heaven.

Gerontius was one of the great and honorable authorities of Rome, who was appointed governor of Caesarea for a long time. He was extremely rich in gold and silver. Gerontius took a Palestinian wife, the daughter of a nobleman. Her name was Theobesta**, and

---

*Anastasius in Coptic/Egyptian. **Theobesta in Coptic/Egyptian, Aklacia in Greek, Bete Kristian in Ge'ez (classical Ethiopian language).

she was also wealthy, possessing much gold, silver, men servant and maid servants. Theobesta was a very holy woman who God chose, and blessed her womb to be the carrier of the star of martyrs, who would illuminate the whole world by his light.

Gerontius and Theobesta had two daughters, Kasia and Mathrona, and one son, George, who was very handsome. His face was like the angel of the Lord, and his stature was excellent in appearance, likened to the splendid trees of Lebanon. Gerontius and Theobesta were Christians who loved God dearly. They gave alms in abundance to the poor, homeless, orphans and widows, therefore everyone loved them greatly because of their kindness. Day and night they prayed and beseeched God in order for Him to lead them in the way of righteousness.

The family of Saint George

Saint George was ten years old when Gerontius died leaving all his wealth; gold, silver, men servants, maidservants, horses, mules, cattle, and sheep to Saint George and his sisters. There was no one in the country of Palestine to be compared with them in riches and charity.

After Gerontius died his position was filled by governor Justus, who was of a good, honorable background, and very rich. He was also a Christian who loved God exceedingly. Justus had one daughter who was five years old. When he became governor he invited everyone to celebrate his coronation, including Saint George and his family. On his coronation day Justus embraced and kissed Saint George, and gave Theobesta a place to sit. He asked Theobesta to give Saint George to him so he could raise him as a son and soldier, as he had no son to take his place when he died, and he also wished to make Saint George a general over his army. Theobesta agreed to the governor's request, and Justus welcomed Saint George, making him leader of one hundred soldiers.

Governor Justus sent Saint George accompanied by a hundred soldiers to the king, who was of a higher rank. Saint George took a letter stating his background; a son of a governor, and honorable ancestors. This was in order that the king could understand how laudable Saint George was, who his parents were, their riches and heritage, and that it was owing to promote this honorable son. When Saint George arrived the king read the letter and greatly rejoiced as he was happy about Saint George. The king promoted him to the rank of captain, leader of five thousand soldiers, with a monthly salary of three thousand dinars of gold. Saint George was sent home with great honor on a finely decorated horse.

When Saint George returned, Governor Justus, all noble men, and the whole country of Lydda welcomed him in a big hall. The next day Theobesta held a big feast for all the people of Lydda; rich, poor, great, small, men, women, children, and she gave much alms to the poor, elders, and orphans. Later she called the governor, his noble men and their armies, and had a feast for three days.

Saint George visits the king who promotes him to army captain.

    Governor Justus signed a letter accepting Saint George as his son, and making him inheritor of all his property, while he Justus was alive, and after his death. After this Saint George had authority over everything the governor possessed.

    Saint George lived with this governor for ten more years.

Saint George finished studying theology, Old and New Testament and military training at the age of twenty. He learned how to be a good horseman, throw spears and hunt. He became a very strong man in all his works. He was a powerful soldier and leader of battle.

There was none to be compared with Saint George by his power, wisdom, beauty, and the grace of God that dwelt with him. Daily grace and power were added to him from God, until people were amazed and wondered about his youthfulness, and the power and wisdom he possessed. When Saint George went to battle all who saw him were scared to fight him. He rode his horse in between his enemies, he entered their cities without fear with his sword in his hand saying, "I am George, powerful and strong, and I come to you with wrath." When they heard his words they threw their swords and spears and all weapons of war from their hands, from the great fear that fell upon them. Saint George always captured his enemies through God's help.

When Saint George was twenty years old, Governor Justus was eager to make a wedding for him and his daughter. He did not know that our Lord Jesus Christ was keeping Saint George to make him a heavenly bridegroom, and a pure virgin. While Governor Justus was on this thought he died by the will of God, and as he signed before, he left all his inheritance to the blessed Saint George.

* * * * * *

After the passing of Governor Justus, Saint George made an official visit to Beirut. There was a great king in that country who built his city beside the sea of Jericho. The wall of the city was as huge as the wall of the country of Rome, with the city gate facing the sea. It was impossible for enemies to enter by land or sea because the city wall was so sturdy.

The people of the country of Beirut were unbelievers who did not know God, their creator. They worshipped a serpent which they called dragon, in which dwelled the spirit of satan. This serpent had wings as an eagle, feet and nails (paw) as a lion, tail as a snake, teeth as a crocodile, and a neck as an ostrich. When this dragon descended into the sea he first looked into the water to see the animals, big and small. He would sink his head into the sea, and expel poisonous venom from his tongue on the sea animals, which would cause their death, and he feasted on their bodies. After this he would come to the dry land, and fly in the air, looking for eagles and other flying creatures, pursuing them. All the animals died once he breathed on them, and their bodies would fall to the land where he would consume them. The dragon would go to the wilderness and devour the animals. Once he saw an animal, the animal could not escape his poison. The same applied to humans who he would catch and eat. There was no escaping this dragon.

The people of Beirut worshipped the dragon as god. Every day the people fed the dragon one girl which was taken from each household by turn. For this reason the dragon did not disturb the people of the city. One day there were no more girls in the city for the dragon to feast on. The people went to the governor threatening to leave the city, as they knew the dragon would want to eat them if they did not provide it with a girl for its daily meal.

The governor told them not to leave as the city would be deserted. The men asked the governor what they should do as they would not give the dragon their wives, without whom they could not survive. The governor told them not to be scared as he would volunteer to give his own daughter to the dragon, as it was now his turn. The people agreed to stay according to the governor's promise.

While the dragon was out that day hunting for food as was customary, the governor's daughter was placed on the tree and left there alone, awaiting the dragon's return.

On this particular day Saint George arrived in Beirut with three of his soldiers. While visiting Beirut, Saint George passed through the dragon's place with his army. He sat down with his soldiers admiring the beauty of the country. Saint George and his soldiers saw the girl tied by rope to the tree. Saint George said to her, "What are you doing here?" The girl replied, "Oh my Lord, they left me here to be eaten by our god the dragon." Saint George was puzzled by her words. "What do you mean? Who is your god, where does he live, what kind of creature is he, and what is his duty?"

The damsel described the dragon to Saint George and told him how the people had to leave a girl for the dragon every day, or the dragon would go to the city and devour everyone. Saint George inquired of the dragon's whereabouts. The girl told Saint George how the dragon hunted animals in the day time, and at sunset he returned to his place, where he would find a girl tied to the tree waiting to be eaten by him. "You also, young man, do not stay here, otherwise he will eat you too."

"I am not afraid of a dragon in which satan dwells!" Saint George exclaimed. The girl responded, "I see you are a young man, even you do not have a beard. Are you more courageous than the people of Beirut who never protected their daughters from the mouth of the dragon, our god?" The blessed Saint George said, "I have a God who created the heaven and the earth, who is omnipotent, and greater that all gods in the earth. He is going to protect me from this cursed dragon!"

While they were talking they saw the dragon approaching from a distance. When the dragon saw that there were other people at the tree with the girl, he took out his tongue and stretched his long neck. He was prepared to fly if Saint George tried to escape. The blessed Saint George who came by the will of God, with the spirit of God, stood up fearlessly when he saw the dragon and made the sign of the cross. The dragon immediately became weak and put his tongue back into his mouth, and his movement became slower.

Saint George came down from his horse, loosened his belt, and placed it around the dragon's neck. He released the girl from the tree, and they went towards the city with the girl leading the dragon by the belt. When they reached the city gate the people were fearful when they saw the dragon. They ran to lock the gate of the city and hide in their houses saying, "Why do you bring this dragon here? Remove it, as it is the one who eats our daughters."

Saint George answered them, "There is no God except our Lord Jesus Christ. If you believe the dragon is your god I will release him and he will eat you up greedily." The people marveled asking Saint George, "Do you have the ability to kill him in order that we can worship your God?" Saint George replied, "Yes, I am going to slay him by the power of our Lord Jesus Christ."

The people agree for Saint George to destroy the dragon and they all gathered to see this. Saint George dismounted his horse, put his belt back on his waist and mounted his horse. He used his spear to take the dragon's life. The people confessed their belief in the God of Saint George. Saint George ordered bishops to come to the city and the people were converted to Christianity. Eleven churches were built, one of which was built on the spot where the dragon was destroyed.

Saint George slaying the dragon

* * * * * * * *

    There was a Persian ruler called Dudianus who defeated the kings of Rome in battle. He became powerful, having authority over the kingdoms of earth. He was an unbeliever in his creator, denying God, and stiff-necked as king Nebuchadnezzar in his time. He blew the wind of idolatry, continually persecuting and opposing the Christians as he destroyed their churches. He wrote a letter of idolatry to the whole world saying:

"I Dudianus, write this letter to my beloved governors who are under my authority. Peace be unto you. I heard about the Christians who try to establish confusion for the sake of one person whose name is Jesus, whose mother's name is Mary. The whole earth is disturbed because of the Christians. Appolon, Polygon, Ardemis, Dias, Eraklis, Ezebel, Armco and Seqmandros and other gods are not worshipped by the Christian. They worship only Christ whom the Jews crucified. Now come to me all of you with your army, authorities, noblemen of the city, captains and scholars, in order to know what I wish to ask of you, and to make council for this matter, in order for all of us to be in one heart before the Christians destroy our kingdom by their magic. For this reason I write this letter to you. Every greatness and peace be to your kingdom."

Five years after this letter arrived to all nations, sixty nine governors who worshipped idols gathered with their armies and officials, along with great multitude of people until the earth was shaking from the enormity of their armies and horses. When they arrived all the governors gave gifts to Dudianus and worshipped him. After Dudianus saw this he was filled with arrogance, and his heart overflowed with conceit. He felt superior, and he started to roar like a lion. He made a feast for seventy days and he sat feasting with the governors. There was no work, no judgment, just feasting for seventy days.

At the end of the seventy feast days Dudianus sat on the throne of judgment in the courtyard to make a decree to the earth. This unbeliever, foolish Dudianus, sat on his throne as king of kings. The governors, and all noblemen sat on his left and right side. He set up seventy idols and he called them gods. These seventy governors, (Dudianus together with the sixty nine governors) worshipped these idols, and Dudianus ordered everyone in the kingdom to worship the idols and offer animal sacrifice.

After this the governors prepared places, and different types of instruments for torturing Christians. They had horses ready to drag the Christians through the streets who did not worship their idols. For three years the Christian were silent, because they feared the great persecution that would come upon them for declaring their belief in Christ.

Dudianus called an assembly in the city of Tyre. Saint George heard of this meeting and planned to go to share his spiritual knowledge, skills, and gain more honor. He did not know that they were gathering to worship idols. He prepared lots of gold, silver and other gifts along with his army. They traveled by ship and arrived in the capital city.

Saint George was surprised to see signs posted throughout the city ordering the persecution of Christians. He realized this city was not the place for him but he decided to stay and face the maltreatment for the sake of his belief in the Lord Jesus Christ. He told his army, "You are dismissed from your services and free to go home. Do not tell my mother that I will face death, and do not go to Lydda, go to another place. Take all these gifts and give alms to the poor." Three of his soldiers who were his closest friends stayed, and recorded the words of Saint George.

Saint George went to the gathering and stood in front of everyone speaking boldly. "I have heard of your wickedness against the Christians in this city. I am a Christian; my Lord is Jesus Christ, Son of God, and Son of Mary." The governors looked at Saint George. "Your appearance is like that of a prince. Who are your parents, what country are you from?" Saint George did not want to tell them his background. "This is the congregation of dogs," he said. "I will not tell my personal history to dogs."

They swore to him by the name of his Lord Jesus Christ, beseeching him to disclose his identity. Since they mentioned his God's name, Saint George told them his family's background, his country and that he ruled over a kingdom. "When I heard you were gathering here I thought it was for a Christian matter so I came to share my knowledge with you, but I found you to be a congregation of dogs."

They tried to deceive him, offering him a high ranking position and riches if he worshipped their idols, but he was not persuaded by their bribes.

He told them, "I am not looking for earthly silver or gold. I carried much wealth to share with you, but I changed my mind and gave it to the poor when I found out about your evil deeds. I will not worship or offer sacrifice to your gods, who are devils, lifeless idols. Your god Apollo cannot be compared to the apostle Peter, who our Lord gave the keys to the kingdom of heaven, neither can he be compared to the great prophet Elijah, who was an angel of God on earth, and taken to heaven in a chariot of fire. None of your gods can be compared to the saints and righteous."

The governors asked Saint George to deny his true faith. They tried to convince him but he refused all their vain propositions with pride. Then the governors decided to torture him severely because he refused to denounce his faith, and worship their idols. They brought out a wooden horse from the torture chamber and hanged Saint George on the wooden horse until his bones were sticking out. After that they lashed him and put salt and vinegar on his torn up flesh.

Dudianus ordered iron boots to be placed on Saint George's feet, and nailed through his soles. They tried forcing Saint George to walk, however, he was unable to do so because of the severity of his pain. Dudianus continued to torture him in various ways. Saint George was beaten on the head with iron nails until his skull was broken.

The Lord Jesus Christ appeared to Saint George and told him that he would be with him and strengthen him through his afflictions, and he would triumph over the wicked governors. He

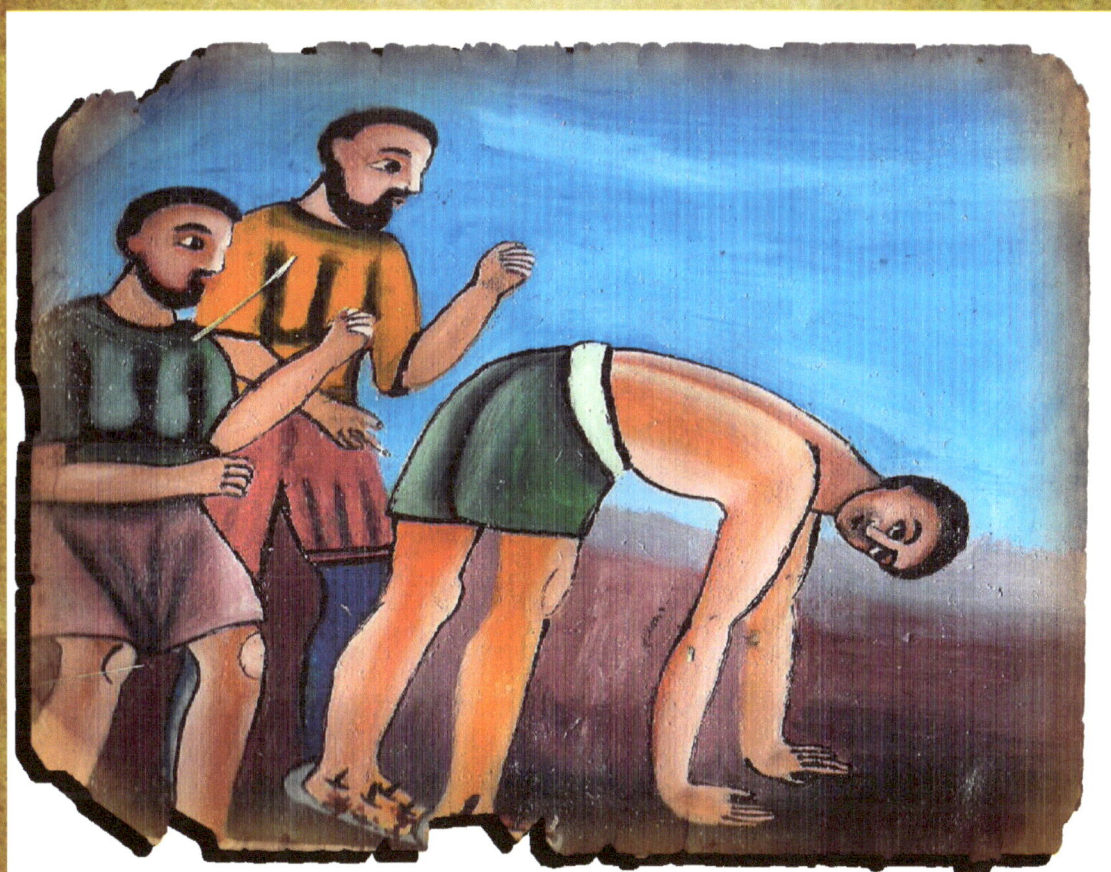
Saint George wearing iron shoes nailed to the soles of his feet.

told him that he would die three times and come back to life, and on his fourth death he would be taken to heaven. God strengthened

Saint George through all his tribulations, which he bore patiently.

When Dudianus saw that Saint George had recovered from all these tortures, and was singing praises to God in Psalms, he believed that this must have been possible only through magic. He thought of getting a magician who would be able to destroy Saint George by superior magical powers. Dudianus wrote a letter which was sent throughout the world, offering a big reward to any magician whose power was greater than that of the magic of George, the Christian.

A magician named Athanasius came forward boasting of his great magical powers, and performed magical acts to convince Dudianus of his ability. Athanasius had an ox brought in front of the governors. He whispered some words in its ears, and the ox split in two. Then Athanasius used a pair of scales on which to weigh both halves of the ox, which when placed on the scales were equal in weight.

Athanasius tried his best to overcome Saint George by calling upon demons, and giving the saint a cupful of poison to drink. Saint George made the sign of the cross over the cup, and then drank it. No harm came to him. The magician tried again by giving Saint George a stronger dose of poison, but still he did not die. Upon seeing this miracle, the magician believed in the Lord Jesus Christ and received baptism. Dudianus was angry, and ordered the beheading of Athanasius, who received the crown of martyrdom.

The magician Athanasius giving Saint George a poisonous drink.

    Dudianus was now totally enraged because he was unable to destroy Saint George as he had planned, and had him thrown in prison. The next day Dudianus ordered a special wheel to be made with various knives, and sword blades to cut through human flesh. When Saint George saw this torture instrument, he knew he would not be able to survive this suffering. He lifted his hands to heaven

and prayed to God, giving Him the glory. The body of the saint was severed in ten pieces, and he delivered up his soul for the first time.

Saint George's body being segmented on the torture wheel.

* * * * * * *

Dudianus praised his gods on the death of Saint George, and had his bones thrown in a pit and covered with dirt saying, "The Christian will never be able to find any piece of his body to make a shrine over it." Then there was lightening, thunder, and an earthquake. Our Lord Jesus Christ sent the might angel Michael to gather the pieces of Saint George's body from the pit. Our Lord breathed life back into the body of Saint George, who returned to the city to confess the glory of God.

Upon realizing that Saint George had risen, Dudianus continued persecuting him by having him sit on a chair which had three red hot spears. The sharp spears pierced through his head and shoulders. Saint George suffered great pain. The angel of the Lord appeared and strengthened him.

St. George sitting on red hot spears which pierced through his head and shoulders.

When the people saw the many miracles performed by the saint, and how he was tortured and came back to life, thousands of souls believed in the Lord Jesus Christ. The governors ordered their heads to be cut off. These believers in the God of Saint George received crowns of martyrdom.

Then Dudianus continued brutalizing St. George by having him bound on an iron bed. After that the command was given for lead to be melted into liquid and shoved in Saint George's mouth. Through the help of God, Saint George survived this and various sufferings inflicted by Dudianus.

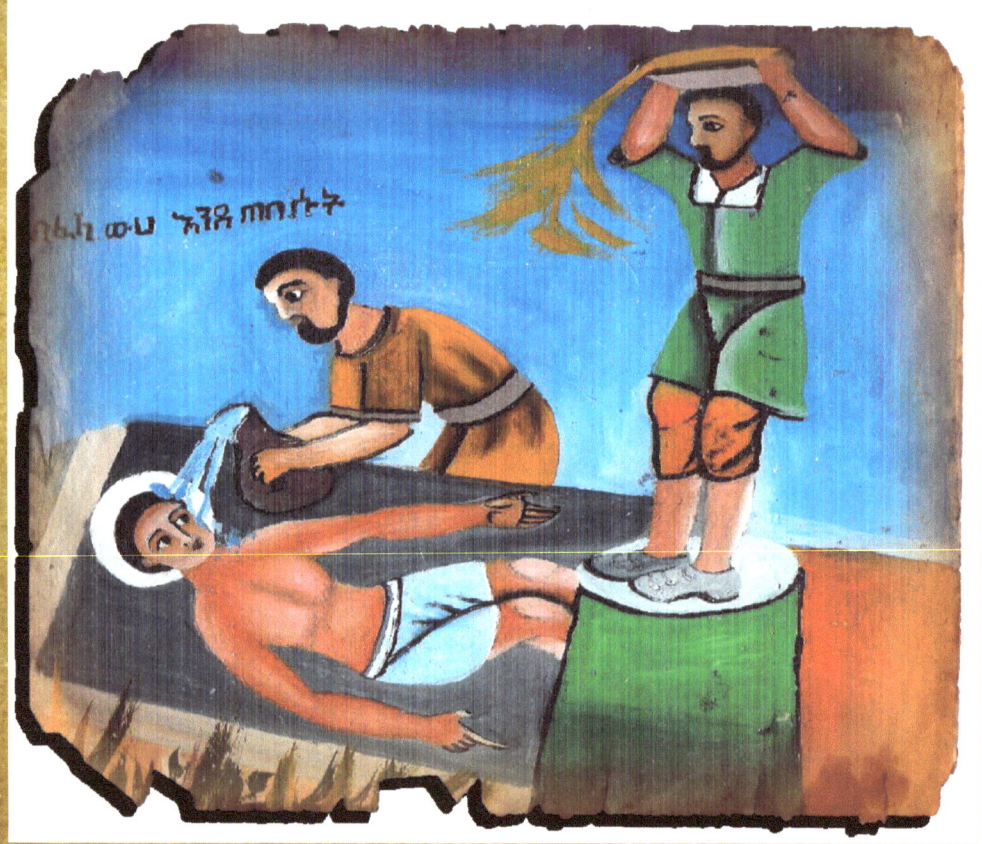

Saint George on an iron bed with melted lead being poured in his mouth.

The next day Dudianus had Saint George brought in front of all the governors. One governor said to Saint George, "I will believe in your God, and worship Him if you can perform a miracle for us to witness." Saint George asked, "What would you like me to do?"

The seventy governors were seated on thrones which had legs made of different types of wood. The governors said to the saint, "We wish you to make these chairs legs produce leaves, and fruits." Saint George prayed and fulfilled the wish. The wood of the chair legs made from fruit bearing trees took roots and brought forth fruits. The wood of the fruitless trees also took roots, bringing forth leaves. When Dudianus saw this miracle he denied the power of the God of Saint George, instead attributing the glory to his god, Apollo.

Saint George miraculously makes hard wooden chairs bear leaves and fruits.

The governor had tried tirelessly to get rid of Saint George without success. He ordered the body of Saint George to be sawed in two and placed with lead in a caldron on a high flame until his body melted. With this the saint gave up his soul for the second time. Dudianus had the remains of Saint George which was in the caldron placed in a pit deep in the earth, so the Christian would not be able to find his body. The Lord sent his angel to bring the body from the pit, and Saint George was again raised from the dead.

Saint George being sawed in two. This was his second death.

* * * * * * *

After Saint George rose from the dead the second time, a poor woman whose name was Scholastike, came and told him about her ox's sudden death, begging the saint for help. The saint prayed and gave her his staff to put on the body of the ox and say, "Saint George says rise up in the name of the Lord Jesus Christ." She did what he told her and the dead ox rose up right away.

Saint George gives his rod to the poor woman to use to raise her dead ox in the name of Jesus Christ.

The governors were puzzled as to how Saint George rose from the dead after his ordeal of death, and burial deep in the earth. They took Saint George to a sepulcher and swore by his gods that if George was able to raise the dead they would accept Christianity.

The governors found only the dust of the bones of the dead, and brought this to Saint George. Saint George knelt down and prayed to the Lord Jesus Christ. When he finished his prayer the Lord raised the dead, among which were five men, and nine women.

The governors were amazed and questioned these people who had raised saying, "How many years ago did you die?" One of the men said, "Over two hundred years." Dudianus questioned him about who he worshipped while he was alive, and if he knew of Christ at that time, and he responded,

> "Every man who lives on earth, and confesses Him whom they crucified, if he bears many sins in his body when he departs from this wicked world, will live in fetters on account of his sins, but on the Lord's day he will have rest because the Lord Jesus looks upon those who are punished on the Lord's day; but as for me, there is no rest at all given to me on the Lord's day because I did not confess Christ's godhead when I lived upon earth. Why then should we confess and worship idols and images which cannot move?" Dudianus the governor answered and said to him, "Thy sense is destroyed through the length of the time of the two hundred years." Then he that had risen from the dead looked upon Saint George the martyr of Christ, and said to him, "O my lord the holy martyr of Christ, we beseech thee to give us thy holy baptism of Christ, that we may not fall back again into the punishment in which we were."[ii]

Saint George smote the earth with his foot, and water sprang up. He baptized them in the name of the Father, the Son, and the Holy Spirit. They returned to their graves, departing in peace to Paradise, leaving Dudianus in amazement.

The other governors said, "It is through magic that this man was able to rise up demons and claim he raised the dead."

Saint George raising the dead.

    The governors imprisoned the saint, chaining him to a pillar in the house of the poorest widow they could find. Saint George was very hungry and he asked the woman for something to eat. She said, "I have no bread." Saint George said, "Who is the god you believe in that you have no bread in your house?" The woman told him she believed in Apollo. When he heard her response, he said, "It is the fair judgment of God that you have no bread in your house." The woman looked on Saint George and saw that his countenance was like that of an angel. She knew that he was a man of God, and she left him in the house to go and ask her neighbors for bread. St. Michael appeared with a table filled with food, and Saint George ate thankfully.

When the widow left, Saint George sat down by a wooden pillar. When his back touched the pillar, the wood took root and grew through the window, becoming a huge tree with lots of fruits. Everyone in the city gathered to watch and partake of the fruits.

The widow returned and saw the great miracles. She fell at the feet of Saint George to worship him but he told her to rise up, as he was only the servant of God, and it was not fitting to worship him as God. The woman then told him, "I have a son who was born blind, deaf, dumb and lame. If you are able to heal my son, I will believe in your God". The woman brought her son to Saint George who prayed over him, and the boy received his sight. The widow said, "I beg you to make him speak, hear and walk." Saint George said, "Woman, for now this is enough. At the appointed time he will hear me when I call him, and he shall go and perform my request".

Dudianus and the sixty nine governors came to the place where the fruit bearing tree had sprung up, and inquired how it got there. They were told it miraculously grew from the place where Saint George sat. Then Dudianus had Saint George brought in front of a crowd of people, and beaten until his flesh was slashed in pieces. After which he had fire placed under Saint George, and continued the torture by hanging the saint up on wood, with pots of fire under him. The flames of the fire were so strong that it destroyed the saint's body, and he gave up his spirit, with his flesh and bones burned to ashes.

Saint George miraculously makes a tree grow from a wooden pillar in a widow's house, and heals her blind son.

* * * * * * *

With the third death of Saint George, the governor ordered his ashes to be cast from a high mountain. The ashes of this saint echoed his name through hills and valleys, "George, George, George." His name was inscribed on leaves on which the ashes fell as it blew in the wind. Then there was lightening, and the mountain was shaken by great thunders. The Lord came upon a cloud of light with his angels, and commanded the four winds of the earth to gather the ashes of Saint George. The Lord commanded Saint George to rise up, embraced him, and the Lord ascended into heaven. When those men who had thrown Saint George over the mountain reached the foot of the mountain, they found St. George there alive sitting on his horse.

Upon seeing how Saint George miraculously came back to life, the men accepted Christ as their Lord, and were baptized. When they returned to the governor and confessed their belief, he had them tortured to death. Saint George was placed in prison until Dudianus decided what should be done to him.

After trying to force Saint George to worship their idols and killing him three times, Dudianus had Saint George brought in front of him saying, "I swear to thee, O George, by the sun, moon and all the God that I will treat you like my beloved son and give you anything you desire, if you will listen to me as a father and agree to worship the gods."

Saint George replied, "I am amazed at these words which you have spoken to me. You have tortured me for the past seven years, killed me three times, and three times my Lord Jesus Christ brought me back to life, but before this moment you have never spoken these words to me since I have been in your authority."

Saint George accepted the governor's invitation to worship his gods. The governor was exceedingly overjoyed and took Saint George to the palace, and left him with Queen Alexander. While Saint George was in the palace, Queen Alexander heard him reading from the 24th Psalm of David, "Why do the heathen reign and the people imagine a vain thing?" The queen inquired of his religion and about whom he read. Saint George explained the Psalm to her, and taught her about the creation, the prophets, and the life of our Lord Jesus Christ up until that moment, and that the idols they were worshipping were not gods. She believed and accepted the Christian faith but asked Saint George not to tell Dudianus until she accepted the crown of martyrdom.

The next morning the governor ordered the people of the city to gather in the temple to witness Saint George offering sacrifice to Apollo and the other gods. Many Christians were sad, and the widow whose son had been healed from blindness cried, wondering how Saint George could do this and dishonor the Christian race.

The idols were brought into the arena in front of the seventy governors and other nobles who came to see Saint George worshiping the idols. Saint George prayed, called the widow's boy and told him to tell the demons to come out of the idols. Immediately the boy's legs were healed and he walked over to the idols. He was able to talk, and commanded the demons to come out and they became physically visible. A demon spoke out saying,

"O master, and saint of God, thou art not ignorant that of old time God made a paradise in Eden, towards the east, and that God put in it the man He had made in His own likeness. And God said, "Let the angels come and worship him;" and straight way Michael and all his army of angels came and worshipped him. But I would not worship the man whom God had created, and I disputed the command of God, saying, "O righteous judge, whom the Cherubim full of eyes overshadow, how can I who am more excellent than this man, worship that which is inferior to me ?"

The widow's son bringing the demon to Saint George.

Then God was very wroth with me, and He cast me forth from the glory with which I was surrounded, and He cast me forth from heaven like an eagle on a rock, and I was in fetters; and now I live in this idol, and I led astray the children of men. And I fly and mount up to the firmament of heaven, and I hear the angels praising God, and when I hear the sentence pronounced that a man shall die and go forth from this world, I go to him and inflict sufferings upon him until he blasphemes God." [iii]
After the demon was finished declaring his true identity,

Saint George prayed and the earth opened and swallowed all the demons that had lived in the idols. Many people immediately believed in the God of Saint George. The governor was angry saying, "I gathered you here to worship the idols not the God of the Christians!"

The governor went to the palace and the queen asked him why he was so furious. "This man George has made a mockery of me, he did not come to worship the idols but destroyed them, and converted the people to his faith!" said Dudianus angrily. The queen answered him saying, "I told you several times not to fight him. He is the servant of the Almighty God." When the governor realized that Queen Alexander had also become a believer in the God of Saint George he dragged her by her hair and brought her to the sixty nine governors. They all agreed to torture her, after which she was beheaded. She too received the crown of martyrdom.

By then Dudianus was humiliated by Saint George, and had grown tired of being unable to defeat him. He decided to have Saint George sentenced to death. He put this in writing, signed it, and had the sixty nine governors sign as well.

Saint George came to the place of his martyrdom with rejoicing. He lifted his eyes to heaven in prayer, and as he prayed fire came down from heaven and consumed the seventy governors who had persecuted him for seven years, along with their assembly who were gathered there.

Saint George prayed to God as they approached to take his body, saying, "Hear the prayer O Lord, of all the people who do good deeds in my name, and forgive them their sins for my sake." The Lord promised Saint George that he would remember everyone who did charitable acts in the name of Saint George, and forgive their

Our Lord Jesus Christ making a covenant with St. George that he would receive the crown of martyrdom, inherit eternal and become the Prince of Martyrs.

sins. The Lord assured Saint George of the great honor, and seven crowns of glory awaiting him in heaven. With this the final martyrdom of Saint George was carried out. Blood, water, and milk flowed from the saint's neck.

After his martyrdom, two of the disciples of Saint George took his body from Persia to the city of Lydda, his hometown, and they built a great church there in his name.

Once a Bishop whose name was Theodotus doubted what is written in the biography of St. George, which says, "There is no one like Saint George among the martyrs, he is the Prince of Martyrs."

Fire descending from heaven on the governors (left). St. George receiving final martyrdom and seven crowns.

One night this bishop saw a vision of Saint George riding his white horse, and all the saints were worshipping the saint next to our Lord. Among these saints was St. Abib, one of the martyred

monks, who explained to Bishop Theodotus about Saint George's very great honor. Then Bishop Theodotus believed fully in his heart what is said about Saint George.

The body of St. George being carried by his disciples for burial.

Bishop Theodotus visions St. George with St. Abib and the Archangel Michael.

Thanks be to God. The prayers and blessing of Saint George be with us forever and ever, Amen.

Here I stand in St. George Greek Orthodox Church in Lod, wearing the chain which is there as a memory of the anguish St. George endured.

The tomb of St. George in Lod, Israel.

Prayer to Saint George

Draw me out of the pit of perdition,

You who rescued the girl from Beirut from

The mouth of the dragon.

Rescue my soul from a murderous enemy.

Preserve the rest of my life from every temptation.[iv]

---

[i] Gebreselassie, T. (1984). *Gelde Giorgis*. Addis Ababa: Tesfa Gebreselassie Printing.
[ii] Budge, E.A.W. (2007). *The Martyrdom and Miracles of Saint George of Cappadocia.* Whitefish, MT: Kessinger Publishing. (Original work published 1888)
[iii] Budge, E.A.W. (2007). *The Martyrdom and Miracles of Saint George of Cappadocia.* Whitefish, MT: Kessinger Publishing. (Original work published 1888)
[iv] Heldman, M., Munro-Hay, S. (1996). *African Zion: The Sacred Art of Ethiopia.* New Haven, CT: Yale University Press.

www.ingramcontent.com/pod-product-compliance
Lightning Source LLC
Chambersburg PA
CBHW042020150426
43197CB00002B/81